CONTENTS

Words that appear in the text in bold, **like this**, are explained in the Glossary.

MACEDONIA

MOUNT OLYMPUS

AEGEAN SEA

THEATRE OF DIONYSUS

ITHACA

Delphi

Chalcis

Thebes

Marathon

OLYMPIC GAMES AT OLYMPIA

Corinth

Olympia

Mycenae

Athens

Argos

ACROPOLIS

Sparta

Europe

ANCIENT GREECE

Italy

Eastern Asia

SEA OF CRETE

Africa

Mediterranean Sea

CRETE

Knossos

MAP OF ANCIENT GREECE

Troy

ESBOS

Ephesus

Miletus

ASIA MINOR

RHODES

MEDITERRANEAN SEA

This is Mount Parnassus. It is a mountain in central Greece.

CHAPTER 1

FACTS ABOUT ANCIENT GREECE

Ancient Greece is one of the ancient world's top places to go on holiday. It has thrilling theatres, exciting sporting events, beautiful buildings, and great art. It also has good weather, beautiful beaches, and tasty food!

Read on to find out what to do, what to wear, and what you'll eat. Our useful tips will have you feeling at home in no time at all!

WHEN TO VISIT

Ancient Greece is a great place, but the ancient Greeks have a lot of wars. You should choose your time to visit carefully. You don't want to get caught up in a bloody battle!

WAR AND WEAPONS

The ancient Greeks fight a lot. They have some of the best **armour** and weapons in the ancient world. They wear armour to protect them when they fight.

Greek soldiers fight in a tight battle formation. This is called a phalanx.

A Greek foot soldier from the 5th century BC.

GOOD TIMES

Each city in ancient Greece has its own leader or group of leaders. The best time to visit ancient Greece is around 478–430 BC. (BC means the years before our modern calendar started.) That was about 2,500 years ago. There is no war in Athens. Athens is the most famous city in Greece.

ANCIENT GREECE – WHEN TO VISIT

(Note: dates given are approximate. BC means the years before our modern calendar started.)

3000 BC	Minoans develop villages on the island of Crete.
1450 BC	Mycenaeans grab power from the Minoans.
1250 BC	Greek armies attack the city of Troy. The war is called the Trojan War.
740 BC	The city of Sparta begins attacking other cities.
546 BC	Persians begin attacking Greece.
490 BC	Greeks beat Persians at the Battle of Marathon.
478 BC	Athens begins "golden age" of learning and art.
445 BC	Athens makes peace with the city of Sparta.
431–421 BC	War between Athens and the city of Sparta.
430 BC	Deadly **plague** (disease) hits Athens.
413–404 BC	Sparta fights and takes control of Athens.
395–387 BC	Several Greek cities and the Persians fight Sparta.
362 BC	Sparta and Athens join forces to fight Thebes.
338 BC	King Philip II takes control of Greece.
336–323 BC	Alexander the Great rules many lands. Alexander is the son of Philip.

When to visit:

Stay away – danger!　　　　　Best time to visit – go for it!

Okay time to visit

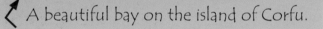

↖ A beautiful bay on the island of Corfu.

GEOGRAPHY AND CLIMATE

Ancient Greece is on the Mediterranean Sea. Travellers like to visit Greece because of its warm, dry summers.

There are many great civilizations near the Mediterranean, like ancient Greece. A civilization is when people have laws (rules) to help them live together. Experts think the warm weather helps these civilizations. It is easy to grow crops and find shelter.

People have time to develop things such as art. They have time to develop ways to run the city.

LOCAL PRODUCE

Greece has plenty of good land for growing crops. Ancient Greek farmers grow mainly wheat, vegetables, and olive trees. They also grow grapes for wine.

Farmers keep pigs, chickens, sheep, and goats. They keep bees for honey, too. The ancient Greeks use honey or boiled grape juice instead of sugar.

EARTHQUAKES AND VOLCANOES

A visit to ancient Greece could be exciting! Greece is an earthquake and volcano zone. You might get shaken or have to dodge **lava**. This is the red-hot liquid rock that comes out of volcanoes!

Mount Thera is the greatest volcano in ancient Greece. It is on the island of Thera. The volcano **erupted** (shot out lava) about 3,630 years ago. It completely destroyed the centre of the island. The eruption was one of the most powerful in history.

Ancient Greece's most famous earthquake happened about 3,710 years ago. It destroyed the Minoan palace of Knossos. Knossos is on the island of Crete.

CLOTHES AND FOOD

Try to fit in with the locals. Dress like the ancient Greeks and change your hairstyle!

WHAT TO WEAR

Men and boys wear a short knee-length tunic. This is made from a piece of light wool or linen (cloth). It has a belt to hold it in place. Women and girls wear longer tunics wrapped around the body. Rich people might have a cotton or silk tunic. The tunic is printed with patterns. Many people go barefoot, or wear leather shoes or sandals.

HOW TO DO YOUR HAIR

Women and girls decorate their hair with ribbons and jewellery. Most men and boys have short hair. Men have a trimmed beard.

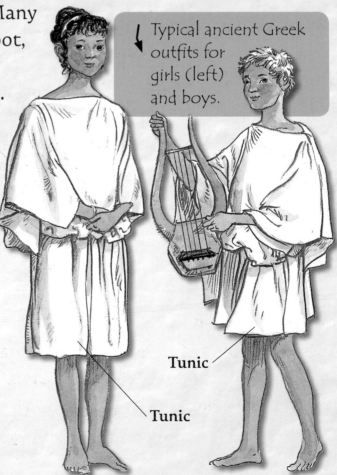

Typical ancient Greek outfits for girls (left) and boys.

Tunic

Tunic

WHAT'S FOR DINNER?

Everyone eats lots of porridge or bread. Bread is made from wheat or barley. They eat fruit and vegetables. They eat figs, apples, pears, plums, and cherries. They eat onions, peas, carrots, and spinach. There is plenty of fresh seafood, such as octopus.

Some ancient Greeks go out and hunt hares, deer, and pigeons. They also collect their own mushrooms and berries.

Everyone drinks wine mixed with water — even the children! Dessert is usually fruit or honey cake.

This carving shows a young woman's decorated hairstyle. It is from about 500 BC. That is 2,500 years ago.

HONEY CAKE

Lots of people eat honey cake. It is made with honey, sesame seeds, and nuts. People like to eat fruit with their honey cake.

PEOPLE

There are some very rich people in Ancient Greek cities. There are also some very poor people.

CITIZENS

A **citizen** is a full member of society. Citizens can vote for leaders. Citizens can own property. In Athens, most citizens are men born in the city.

WOMEN

Ancient Greece is a **sexist** society. In ancient Greece people think that men are more important than women. Women belong to their male relatives.

Wealthy women have to stay indoors and run the house. Poorer women might work in the fields or in the market. Most girls don't go to school. Most women cannot read or write.

The men in Sparta fight a lot of wars. Women are important there. Women take part in running and other sports. They need to be healthy and able to have strong children. Strong boys become soldiers.

SLAVES

Slaves do all the hard work without getting any pay.
Slaves are owned by other
people. They work
in farms. There
are also slaves
who do the
housework.
Slaves can be
male or female.
Some people
become slaves
as children.
Prisoners from
other lands
become slaves.
So do people
who run away.

This is a wealthy woman in ancient Greece. She is with her slave.

DON'T BE RUDE!

Good manners are important in ancient Greece. Here are some to remember:

- Don't go to the toilet in the street!
- Never laugh at people for being poor. It's not their fault.

COMMUNICATIONS

In ancient Greece there are no phones. There's certainly no Internet. You have to use a messenger to send a message. News travels very slowly.

CODED MESSAGES

The ancient Greeks send secret messages. One way is to tattoo the message on to the messenger's shaved head. They send him once his hair has grown. The messenger shaves his head again to show the message!

A strip of letters reveals a secret message.

The Spartans send messages written on long strips of leather. You have to wrap the strip around a stick of exactly the right size. The letters line up and form words. You can then read the message.

RELIGION

The ancient Greeks have many gods. You'll see temples and statues of gods everywhere.

GODS AND GODDESSES

There are dozens of ancient Greek gods and goddesses. Here are a few of the most important ones:

- **Zeus** – king of the gods. He is the father of many of the younger gods.
- **Hera** – Zeus's wife. She is the goddess of women and marriage.
- **Athena** – goddess of war and wisdom. She also guards over Athens.
- **Apollo** – god of the Sun and light.
- **Artemis** – goddess of the Moon and of hunting.
- **Dionysus** – god of wine, parties, and the theatre.
- **Demeter** – goddess of the Earth, plants, and farming.
- **Aphrodite** – goddess of love and beauty.
- **Asclepius** – god of medicine.
- **Poseidon** – god of the sea. He is known for his terrible temper.
- **Pluto** – god of the Underworld. Souls go here after death.

WHAT CAN THE GODS DO?

The gods can control events and answer prayers. They can do magic and change shape. Ancient Greek gods are not always good and kind. They can be jealous and cruel to people.

This vase painting shows Dionysus, god of wine and parties.

STORIES OF THE GODS

The ancient Greeks have hundreds of stories about their gods and ancient heroes. They tell the stories in poems and plays.

One Greek story is about a beauty competition between three goddesses. They were Aphrodite, Athena, and Hera. The competition was judged by Paris, prince of Troy. Aphrodite won the competition by promising Paris the most beautiful woman in the world. She promised him Helen, the queen of Sparta. The Trojan War began when Paris stole Helen away (see also page 39).

RELIGIOUS FESTIVALS

Most ancient Greek religious festivals include feasts, music, and sports. They also include processions, when lots of people walk through the streets together. There are offerings of food and wine. The ancient Greeks believe that offerings will make the gods happy. Happy gods will help the people. If the ancient Greeks do not make offerings the gods will be unhappy. Unhappy gods may send storms or harm the people in other ways.

Many ancient Greeks have an altar in their home. An altar is a special place. This is where offerings of food or wine are made to the gods.

You can visit an **oracle**. An oracle is a special place where a priestess (female priest) can talk to the gods. Here people are able to ask one of the gods a question.

Part of the oracle of Apollo at Delphi. This is where people from Athens leave their offerings to the god.

The Parthenon temple is the most famous building in Athens.

CHAPTER 2

LEADERS AND GOVERNMENT

Ancient Greece is famous for its government. The government runs the country. Ancient Greece is not a single country with one king or queen. Instead, it is made up of lots of **city-states**. A city-state is a city along with the villages and countryside around it. Each city-state has its own rulers and laws (rules). You must not forget where you are. What is allowed in Athens could be a crime in Sparta!

ALL ABOUT ATHENS

Athens is the most important of all the **city-states**. Artists, writers, and scientists come here from all over the Mediterranean.

Athens has a long history. It has become the most powerful city in ancient Greece. This happened 2,500 years ago. Athens started as a small settlement. A settlement is a group of people living in houses close together. The small settlement was started around 3,400 years ago.

The first Athenians lived on top of a high hill. This was the safest place to watch out for enemies. The rest of the city grew around this hilltop area. This became known as the **Acropolis**. An acropolis is part of a city built on a hill.

The Acropolis in Athens as it looks today.

TAKING CONTROL

Athens won a lot of battles against other city-states. It grew rich from the nearby silver mines. It became a centre for travel and trade.

THE NAMING OF ATHENS

Athens is named after the goddess Athena. According to an ancient Greek story, Athena and Poseidon both wanted to be the god of the city.

Athena offered the people a gift of an olive tree. Poseidon offered the gift of a well. The well's water was as salty as the sea. The people decided Athena's gift of an olive tree was far more useful. Athena became the city's goddess.

The statue of Athena inside the Parthenon.

HANGING OUT

Athens has lots of theatres and libraries. It has lots of gymnasiums and shops. **Citizens** like to discuss their leaders. They like to discuss plays and parties.

THE ACROPOLIS

Most **city-states** have an **acropolis**. This hilltop area is usually the oldest part of town. The Acropolis in Athens is the most famous of all. It is full of temples and statues.

DEMOCRACY

Some city-states are ruled by **tyrants** or kings. Tyrants are strict rulers who took power. But there's a new system in Athens, called **democracy**. It means ruled by the people. It comes from the Greek words *demos* meaning "people" and *kratos* meaning "power".

SPARTA

Sparta is very different from Athens. The Athenians like art, culture, and parties. The Spartans care only about fighting. Adults train their children to be tough fighters by beating them.

Only citizens can vote, though. Citizens are free men born in Athens. This means that many people are left out. This includes women and **slaves**.

In ancient Greek democracy, the citizens can also take part in decisions. They go to a big public meeting. This is called the Assembly. At the Assembly they can vote on new laws. They can vote on how to spend money. People vote by holding up their hand or a stick.

Greeks enjoy gathering in public places to listen to speakers.

This picture of a Greek warship was painted around 2,500 years ago.

CHAPTER 3

TRAVEL, FOOD, AND SHELTER

Ancient Greece is a big place, so you will need transport to get around. On land you might travel by **chariot**. A chariot is a kind of cart pulled by animals. You will need to travel by ship if you visit some of the islands. You may be able to stay in someone's house. This is the best way to find out how the ancient Greeks live.

ON THE MOVE

Most people travel on foot. There are no cars, buses, trains, or bicycles.

TRAVEL BY LAND

The ancient Greeks use horses and donkeys. You can even ride in a horse-drawn **chariot** or carriage. Or you can just ride the horse itself. But there are no saddles, just blankets and reins.

TRAVEL TIPS

Follow these handy travel tips to stay safe on the road.
- Don't travel during wars — you could get killed!
- Watch out for bandits. Bandits wait for travellers and rob them.

A vase painting showing a horse-drawn chariot in a wedding procession.

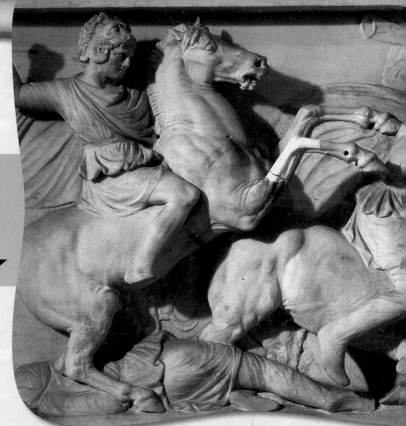

A carving shows Alexander the Great riding his horse bareback into battle. ➜

TRAVEL BY SEA

The quickest way to travel in ancient Greece is by boat. The ancient Greeks travel from one place to another around the coast. They also use ships to travel between the Greek islands. They use ships to cross the Mediterranean Sea to other lands.

Some ships have sails to make them move. Some ships are moved by men pulling on oars. Oars are long pieces of wood. They are used to push the boat forward through the water. Some ships have sails and oars.

WHERE TO STAY

On long journeys, you may be able to stay in guesthouses by the roadside. The ancient Greeks believe it is polite to offer food and shelter to travellers. You will probably be able to stay in someone's house.

STEP INSIDE

Most ancient Greek houses are built of mud bricks. There's a special dining room for the men. There are other rooms for women and **slaves**. The bedrooms are usually upstairs. They are reached by a ladder or staircase.

A view inside a typical ancient Greek house.

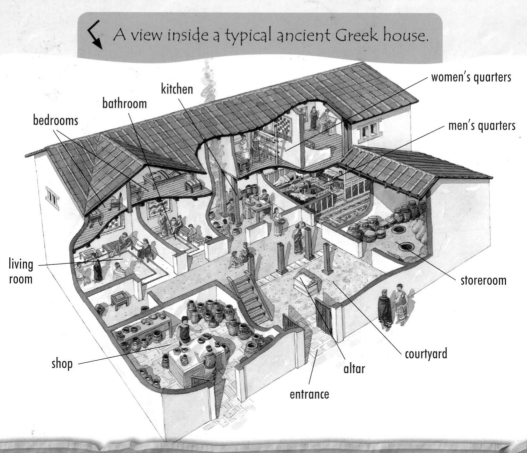

bedrooms

bathroom

kitchen

women's quarters

men's quarters

living room

storeroom

shop

altar

courtyard

entrance

MAKE YOURSELF AT HOME

Bedrooms have cosy beds with proper mattresses and pillows. There are washbasins for keeping clean. Slaves will serve you food and wash your clothes. They will even play you some music. When you leave, it is polite to give your host a thank-you gift. You might give a silver bowl.

A vase painting showing a slave playing the flute for a party guest.

HOW MEN AND WOMEN BEHAVE

Men and boys sit back and have everything done for them by slaves or women. Women and girls do some weaving, or look after babies.

The Odeum is a large theatre in Athens. The ancient Greeks love going to the theatre.

CHAPTER 4

WHAT TO SEE AND DO

There are lots of things to do in ancient Greece. You can watch plays or play sports. You can go exploring or you can just relax. There are lots of beautiful islands and beaches to visit.

THE THEATRE

The ancient Greeks love going to the theatre — and so they should. They invented it!

BOOK NOW!

Plays are shown during the day, while it is still light. You buy your tickets at the theatre as you go in. "Tickets" are pieces of bronze or lead. They are stamped with a letter to show where to sit. Boys can go to the theatre, but not girls.

GREEK THEATRES

Greek theatres are open-air. The most famous theatre in ancient Greece is the Theatre of Dionysus. It is in Athens. It can seat up to 17,000 people.

The layout of a typical Greek theatre.

WHAT TO EXPECT

A typical ancient Greek play has a chorus and three actors. The actors are all men. Each actor plays several parts. Some plays are **tragedies** (plays with sad endings). Some plays are comedies. Comedies make fun of famous people.

Greek theatres are very big, so the view from the back is dreadful. Actors wear masks like these. This means that people sitting at the back can see the emotions on the masks.

Here's a programme guide to two Greek plays:

- *Agamemnon* is a tragedy by Aeschylus. Agamemnon is a Greek hero and battle leader. He returns from the Trojan War, but is murdered by his wife.

- *The Wasps* is a comedy by Aristophanes. It is about an old man who loves law courts. A law court is a place where people are taken if they are accused of a crime. He even takes his dog to court for stealing some cheese.

THE OLYMPIC GAMES

The biggest sports event in Ancient Greece is the Olympic Games. This is held every four years.

A 21st century view of the running track at Olympus.

GOING TO THE GAMES

The Olympic Games are held at Olympia. Olympia is about 325 kilometres (200 miles) from Athens. The games are very important. Wars stop during them!

The Games last five days, with many different kinds of sports to watch. Athletes take part in foot races, chariot races, and jumping contests. There are also throwing events such as discus and javelin. A javelin is like a spear.

OLYMPIC EVENTS

- **Foot race** – running up and down a track called a *stade*. (The word "stadium" comes from stade.)
- **Wrestling** – two wrestlers try to force each other to the ground.
- **Discus** – throwing a very heavy metal or stone disc.
- **Javelin** – throwing a spear.
- **Chariot race** – races for chariots drawn by two or four horses.
- **Pentathlon** – a contest of five events: foot race, long jump, discus, javelin, and wrestling.

GAMES FOR WOMEN

Women can't take part in the Olympics. There is a separate sports contest for women. Married women are not allowed to watch the men's games. Younger girls can. It is a really good place to meet a future husband.

PRIZES

Each winning athlete gets a prize of a crown of laurel leaves. He usually also gets a cash reward from his **city-state**. A cheating athlete is whipped in public.

A sculpture of an athlete about to throw the discus.

THE HISTORY TRAIL

Ancient Greeks love to look back on the even more ancient past. They see this as a time of magic and mystery.

THE MYSTERIOUS MINOANS

Take a trip to Crete. Crete is Greece's largest island. The Minoans lived on Crete about 4,000 years ago. They lived there for almost 1,000 years. They built a huge palace called Knossos.

A Roman mosaic showing Theseus wrestling with the Minotaur.

A MONSTER THAT EATS CHILDREN

There is a Greek story about the Minotaur. This was a monster with a man's body and a bull's head (see above). It lived beneath the palace at Knossos in a great maze. Every nine years, King Minos forced the people of Athens to send seven boys and seven girls for the Minotaur to eat. Theseus was a prince of Athens. He went to Crete and killed the Minotaur.

THE MIGHTY MYCENAEANS

People called the Mycenaeans came to power from about 1500 BC. That was about 3,500 years ago. Mycenae was their capital city. The Mycenaeans feature in many ancient Greek stories.

The ruins of graves at Mycenae.

TROY

The greatest ancient Greek story is about the city of Troy. Paris was a prince of Troy. He ran away with Helen, a Greek queen. The Greeks tried to get her back by sailing to Troy. They attacked the city for 10 years, and finally destroyed it. The ruins of Troy have been found in what is now the country of Turkey.
Archaeologists are people who study the past. Archaeologists believe the Trojan War really did happen. They think it happened almost 3,200 years ago.

MORE THINGS TO DO

GO TO THE GYM

If you're male, you can go to a gymnasium. Men go there to exercise, bathe, and chat with friends. There are spaces for public baths, running, and sports training. There are also rooms for making speeches and discussing things.

ART AND ARCHITECTURE

Make sure you visit ancient Greece at the right time. You should go after all the most famous buildings have been built!

- The Temple of Zeus at Olympia was built around 465 BC. That was about 2,475 years ago.
- The Parthenon in Athens was built around 440 BC. That was about 2,450 years ago. It is a temple dedicated to the goddess Athena.

Corinthian columns on a temple in Athens.

KNOW YOUR COLUMNS!

Greek temples often have columns at the front. This drawing shows the three styles.

The three types of ancient Greek columns.

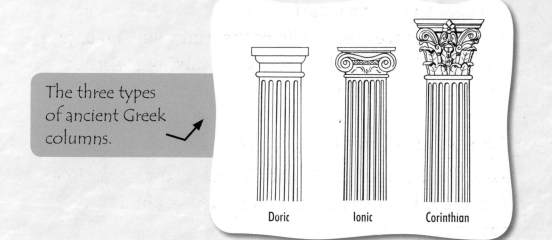

Doric   Ionic   Corinthian

GAMES

Ancient Greeks often pass the time playing games such as dice, juggling, and marbles.

This vase painting shows ancient Greeks playing a game.

A pair of ancient Greek gold earrings from about 400 BC. That was about 2,400 years ago.

CHAPTER 5

SHOPPING, HEALTH, AND SAFETY

There are plenty of things to buy in the markets. You can buy beautiful jewellery, silver, and pottery vases. The ancient Greeks make all these themselves. They also bring things from other countries. They bring things like perfume, ivory, and precious stones.

Make sure you stay healthy and safe! This chapter will tell you about Greek medicine and how to avoid being robbed.

THE MARKETPLACE

Every town and city has a marketplace. Here farmers and traders bring their goods to sell. People go there to meet friends or have a snack. They also go to tell each other what is happening.

GREEK CURRENCY

Here's a guide to Greek currency for when you go shopping. The basic unit is the **drachma**. In 440 BC a skilled worker might earn about 1 drachma a day.

1 drachma = 6 obols	100 drachmas = 1 mina
1 obol = 12 chalkoi	60 minas = 1 talent

In most towns, the market is held in a big, open central square. The traders set up their stalls around the sides. Stalls are tables where the traders show the things they are selling. People come to their stalls to buy things.

SLAVES FOR SALE

Most marketplaces have a platform. The platform is a high area that slaves stand on. The slaves are bought and sold here. The price of a slave depends on how young, healthy, and useful he or she is. Workers also gather at the market to offer themselves for hire.

COINS

The ancient Greeks began using coins in about 600 BC. That was about 2,600 years ago. Each **city-state** issues its own coins. The coins have pictures on them. Get the local coins at a bank before you go to the market. If you can't find any pockets in your tunic, do what the Greeks do. They carry loose change in their mouth!

A silver coin from ancient Athens. It is decorated with an image of the goddess Athena.

WHAT TO BUY

You can buy lots of ordinary things. You can buy food, wine, and tools. You can buy vases and jewellery.

FRESH FOOD

The ancient Greeks come to the marketplace mainly to buy their food. You can buy wheat and barley. You can buy fresh fruit and vegetables. You can buy cheese, fish, and meat. Some animals, such as chickens, are sold alive.

EVERYDAY ITEMS

Traders sell tunics, cloaks, and sandals. They sell wool and cotton cloth. Craftsmen sell the goods they have made. They sell jewellery, furniture, and toys.

An ancient Greek toy soldier on horseback.

TOYS

You'll be able to find toys for your little brother or sister. There are dolls, kites, and pottery toy animals. You can also get toy carts with mini-harnesses. These can attach to your own dog.

PICK UP A POT

The best souvenir of ancient Greece is a painted vase or pot. Many pots are decorated with scenes from stories. Other pots are covered with patterns.

An ancient Greek perfume jar with a female face. ↘

POTTERY GUIDE

Here is a list of some of the different types of pots you can buy.

- **Amphora** – storage jar for wine, oil, or water.
- **Crater** – jug for mixing wine and water.
- **Oinochoe** – jug for wine and water.
- **Hydria** – jar for collecting water.
- **Aryballos** – small perfume jar.

KEEPING HEALTHY

Don't forget to look after yourself! There are **plagues** and other diseases. The human body is very important to the ancient Greeks. They love sport and like to get plenty of exercise.

<ⵌ A carving showing Asclepius caring for a patient.

THE GOD OF MEDICINE

The earliest ancient Greeks think illnesses are caused by the gods. You pray for help to Asclepius, the god of medicine. If you get better, you leave a thank-you offering to Asclepius.

PLAGUE HORROR

Whatever you do, avoid Athens between 430–426 BC. That was about 2,440 years ago. You may pick up a nasty disease called the plague. No one knows how to cure it. A quarter of the population gets wiped out!

ANCIENT GREEK MEDICINE

You can visit a health centre if you are ill. The doctor may give you a medicine made from plants. The Greeks use nettles (a plant) to clean the blood. They use mustard to kill germs. The Greeks can bandage wounds. They even do operations to **amputate** (cut off) limbs. They do not have any painkillers. Just try not to get ill in the first place.

HIPPOCRATES — THE MOST FAMOUS DOCTOR IN ANCIENT GREECE

Hippocrates lived about 2,420 years ago. He believed diseases had natural causes. He started a medical school. He made his students swear the Hippocratic oath. The oath was a promise not to harm their patients. Doctors still swear the Hippocratic oath today.

A marble carving showing the head of Hippocrates.

CRIME AND PUNISHMENT

There are no cameras and no burglar alarms in ancient Greece. It is a lot easier for villains to commit crimes!

CATCHING CRIMINALS

Citizens catch people who have committed small crimes. Citizens can decide the punishment. So if you lose your bag, just ask someone for help. Athens has a small police force made up of **slaves**.

Here are some ancient Greek criminals to watch out for:

- Bandits — they wait by the roadside and rob travellers.
- Pirates — they attack ships and steal the goods.
- Revenge killers — people sometimes take revenge for a crime by murdering someone.
- Robbers — they steal treasures from temples.

ANCIENT GREEK LAW COURTS

Some ancient Greek **city-states** have laws and law courts to punish wrongdoers. A law court is a place where people are taken if they are accused of a crime. A law court has a **jury**. The jury is made of members of the public. They decide if a person is innocent or guilty.

The suspect and witnesses (people who may have seen the crime) make speeches. The members of the jury vote using bronze voting tokens (see below).

The law court also has a **magistrate** (judge). The judge is in charge of the court. The judge decides what the punishment will be if the person is guilty.

PUNISHMENTS

Punishments for crimes include fines or being made a slave. Punishments also include being sent away from the city, or death. The death penalty can be carried out in several horrible ways. These include poisoning or being thrown off a cliff.

The voting token on the left has a solid centre, meaning "not guilty". The one above has a hollow (empty) centre. It means "guilty".

Ancient Greek lettering carved on stone.

CHAPTER 6

ANCIENT GREECE: FACTS AND FIGURES

Use this handy reference section to learn how to read the Greek alphabet and how to say Greek words. You can also look up famous Greeks, and find out about ancient Greek history.

THE GREEK CALENDAR

DAYS OF THE WEEK

The days of the week are named after the Sun, the Moon, and five Greek gods. The seven days are:

Hemera heliou	Day of the Sun	Sunday
Hemera selenes	Day of the Moon	Monday
Hemera Areos	Day of Ares	Tuesday
Hemera Hermu	Day of Hermes	Wednesday
Hemera Dios	Day of Zeus	Thursday
Hemera Aphrodites	Day of Aphrodite	Friday
Hemera Khronu	Day of Cronos	Saturday

MONTHS OF THE YEAR

The ancient Greek calendar has twelve months. They have different names in different parts of Greece. This calendar shows the names used in Athens:

Hekatombaion	June/July
Metageitnion	July/August
Boedromion	August/September
Pyanepsion	September/October
Maimakterion	October/November
Poseideion	November/December
Gamelion	December/January
Anthesterion	January/February
Elaphebolion	February/March
Munychion	March/April
Thargelion	April/May

ANCIENT GREECE PHRASE BOOK

THE GREEK ALPHABET

The ancient Greek alphabet has 24 letters. This guide shows you the lower-case version of each letter. It shows its name, and how to say it.

Letter	Name of letter	How to say it
α	alpha	*a* as in c<u>a</u>t
β	beta	*b* as in <u>b</u>ath
γ	gamma	*g* as in <u>g</u>oat
δ	delta	*d* as in <u>d</u>og
ε	epsilon	*e* as in b<u>e</u>d
ζ	zeta	*z* as in <u>z</u>oo
η	eta	*ay* as in d<u>ay</u>
θ	theta	*th* as in <u>th</u>ink
ι	iota	*i* as in b<u>i</u>n
κ	kappa	*k* as in <u>k</u>itchen
λ	lambda	*l* as in <u>l</u>eg
μ	mu	*m* as in <u>m</u>at
ν	nu	*n* as in <u>n</u>ose
ξ	xi	*ks* as in fo<u>x</u>
ο	omicron	*o* as in h<u>o</u>t
π	pi	*p* as in <u>p</u>ig
ρ	rho	rolled *r* as in <u>r</u>abbit
σ	sigma	*s* as in <u>s</u>it
τ	tau	*t* as in <u>t</u>oe
υ	upsilon	between <u>ee</u> and <u>oo</u>
φ	phi	*f* as in <u>f</u>oot
χ	chi	*ch* as in lo<u>ch</u>
ψ	psi	*ps* as in chi<u>ps</u>
ω	omega	*o* as in h<u>o</u>me

USEFUL ANCIENT GREEK WORDS, PHRASES, AND NUMBERS

English	Ancient Greek	How to say it
Hello/Goodbye	*Khaire*	Chay-re
Thank you	*Kharis soi*	Cha-ris soy
Excuse me	*Sungignô'ske moi*	Sun-gig-know-ske moy
How can I help?	*Ti d' ou mellô?*	Ti doo mellow?
No thank you	*Ma'lista*	Mal-ist-a
Cheers! (I drink your health!)	*Propinô soi*	Pro-pee-know soy
Where?	*Pou?*	Poo?
When?	*Pote?*	Pott-eh?

Numbers	Ancient Greek
1	|
2	||
3	|||
4	||||
5	Γ
6	Γ|
7	Γ||
8	Γ|||
9	Γ||||
10	Δ

GREAT ANCIENT GREEKS

(BC means the years before our modern calendar started.)

Aesop

Aesop lived before the 6th century BC. That is over 2,600 years ago. Aesop was a slave who made up **fables** (stories). He lived on the island of Samos. We don't know much else about him.

Alexander the Great

Alexander lived from 356 to 323 BC. That is about 2,350 years ago. Alexander was the son of Philip II, the king of Macedonia. Alexander was a famous soldier. He took control of most of ancient Greece. This happened after his father was murdered. Alexander also took control of Persia and many other lands. He died when he was only 32 years old.

Archimedes

Archimedes lived from 287 to 212 BC. That is about 2,260 years ago. Archimedes was a great scientist and inventor. He studied space and science. He invented the Archimedes screw for lifting water. He also invented many weapons to help defend the town of Syracuse. Syracuse is in Italy.

Aristophanes

Aristophanes lived from 445 to 385 BC. That was about 2,420 years ago. He wrote plays. Most of his plays were comedies.

Aristotle

Aristotle lived from 384 to 322 BC. That was about 2,360 years ago. Aristotle was a scientist, **philosopher** (thinker), and writer. He wrote about many things. He wrote about animals and plants. He wrote about space, weather, and much more.

Euripides

Euripides lived from 485 to 406 BC. That was about 2,450 years ago. He wrote plays. His most famous plays were **tragedies** (sad stories).

Herodotus

Herodotus lived from about 460 to 370 BC. That was about 2,400 years ago. Herodutus studied history. His writings tell us a lot about ancient Greek wars. He also wrote about people and the way they lived.

Homer

Homer probably lived sometime in the 8th century BC. That is about 2,800 years ago. Homer was a great poet. In Homer's day, poets recited (spoke) their poems. The poems were only written down much later.

Pericles

Pericles lived from about 495 to 429 BC. That was about 2,470 years ago. Pericles controlled Athens for 14 years. He ordered the Parthenon temple to be built. He also made many new laws.

Plato

Plato lived from 427 to 347 BC. That was about 2,400 years ago. Plato was a philosopher (thinker). He studied with Socrates. Plato started a school called The Academy.

Pythagoras

Pythagoras lived from about 580 to 500 BC. That was about 2,550 years ago. Pythagoras was a philosopher (thinker) and mathematician. He made several important mathematical discoveries.

Sappho

Sappho lived from around 610 to 550 BC. That was about 2,600 years ago. Sappho was a poet. She is famous for her short love poems. Only a few pieces of her work remain.

Socrates

Socrates lived from 469 to 399 BC. That was about 2,450 years ago. Socrates was a great philosopher (thinker). He discussed ideas with his friends and followers in Athens. His followers wrote his ideas down later.

Sophocles

Sophocles lived from around 496 to 405 BC. That was about 2,450 years ago. Sophocles lived in Athens. He wrote plays. He was famous for his tragedies. Sophocles was the first writer to use three actors.

ANCIENT GREECE AT A GLANCE

TIMELINE

(Note: dates given are approximate. BC means the years before our modern calendar started.)

BEFORE 3000 BC	**PREHISTORIC GREECE**
40,000 BC	Early cave people live in the area that will become ancient Greece.
6000 BC	People settle on the island of Crete.
5000 BC	Mediterranean peoples begin farming (instead of just hunting and gathering food).
4000 BC	People settle on the Greek islands.
3000–1100 BC	**THE BRONZE AGE**
3000 BC	The Minoan **civilization** (complex society) develops on the island of Crete.
1600 BC	Mycenaean culture grows on mainland Greece.
1450 BC	The Mycenaeans destroy Minoan palaces.
1250 BC	The Mycenaeans fight the Trojan War against Troy.
1200 BC	Many Greeks leave Greece and settle in other lands.
1100 BC	Mycenae becomes less important.

1100–800 BC **THE DARK AGE**

During this time, Greek culture dies out and the art of writing is lost.

800–500 BC **THE ARCHAIC PERIOD**

The word archaic means "old".

800 BC	The ancient Greeks start using a new writing system.
776 BC	Date of the first recorded Olympic Games.
700 BC	Greeks set up new cities around the Mediterranean.
621 BC	Draco writes a strict set of new laws for the city of Athens.
600 BC	Coins are used in Greece for the first time.
546 BC	The Persians start to invade and conquer parts of Greece.
507 BC	Athenian leader Cleisthenes introduces early **democracy** (when citizens can vote to decide how to run the city).

500–323 BC	**THE CLASSICAL PERIOD**
490 BC	The Greeks defeat Persia at the Battle of Marathon.
479 BC	The Greeks beat the Persians and kick them out of Greece.
449 BC	Greece and Persia make a peace pact.
440–430 BC	Athens is at the height of its "golden age" of culture.
445 BC	Athens makes a peace deal with its neighbour Sparta.
431–404 BC	Peloponnesian Wars between Athens and Sparta.
430–426 BC	An outbreak of the **plague** hits Athens and Sparta.
404 BC	Sparta finally defeats and conquers Athens.
395–340 BC	Battles between Sparta and other Greek **city-states**.
338 BC	King Philip II of Macedonia takes over most of Greece.
336–423 BC	Alexander the Great, Philip's son, rules Greece and conquers Persia and many other lands.

323–30 BC	**THE HELLENISTIC AGE**

The period of history before the Romans took over ancient Greece.

323–148 BC	The Greek city-states fight each other after Alexander's death.
Around 200 BC	The Romans begin to attack and invade Greece.
146 BC	The Romans rule most of Greece.

FURTHER READING

BOOKS

Eyewitness: Ancient Greece, Anne Pearson (Dorling Kindersley, 2004)

Horrible History: The Groovy Greeks, Terry Deary (Scholastic, 1995)

The Usborne Internet-linked Encyclopedia of Ancient Greece, Lesley Miles (Usborne, 2003)

GLOSSARY

acropolis part of a city built on a high hill and surrounded by strong walls. The word means "high town".

amputate cutting off an arm or a leg if it is too badly wounded or infected

archaeologist someone who studies the past, using information from old books, ruins, and other objects

armour leather or metal covering for the body. Soldiers wear armour to protect them when they fight.

chariot kind of cart pulled by an animal

citizen in ancient Greece, a full member of society, who can vote and own property

city-state independent state made up of a city and the land and villages around it. Each city-state has its own rulers and laws.

civilization complex society with cities, art, and culture

democracy rule by the people, from the Greek words *demos* meaning people and *kratos* meaning power

drachma the basic unit of currency in ancient Greece

erupt when a volcano shoots out lava (hot, molten rock)

fable a story that teaches a lesson. Many fables are about animals that can talk.

jury members of the public who vote on whether someone standing trial is innocent or guilty

lava hot, molten rock that comes out of volcanoes

magistrate type of judge

oracle religious place where people can go to ask the gods questions

philosopher thinker. Someone who has lots of ideas about the nature of the world.

plague a disease that killed many people

sexist treating people unfairly on the basis of whether they are male or female

slave a person who is owned by someone else. Slaves usually have to work very hard and get no pay

tragedy type of play dealing with serious and sad events

tyrant ruler who has complete control, often after seizing power

INDEX